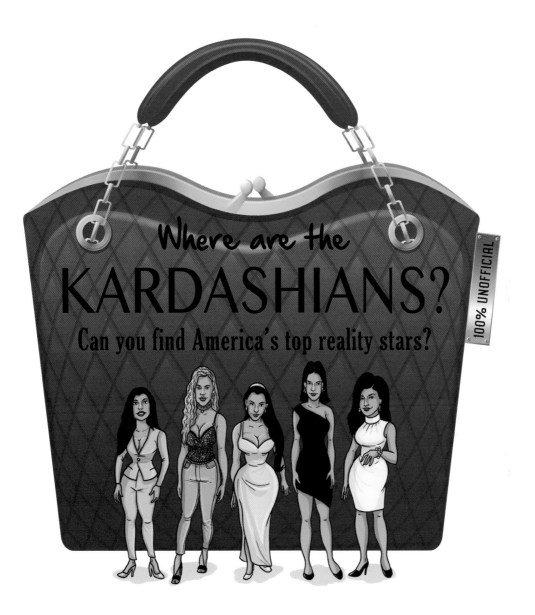

Where are the
KARDASHIANS?

Can you find America's top reality stars?

100% UNOFFICIAL

igloobooks

Where are the
KARDASHIANS?

Can you find America's top reality stars?

Successful and stylish, the Kardashian-Jenner family became reality superstars with the hit TV show, *Keeping Up with the Kardashains*. Alongside their extended family and celebrity friends, these glamorous girls have been the focus of global fascination and envy for over a decade.

When it comes to business, fashion, and luxury, savvy sisters Kourtney, Kim, Khloe, Kendall, and Kylie, led by their 'momager' Kris, have shown the world how it's done. But just how is it done? Explore ten scenes depicting the Kardashian lifestyle to see if you can find out!

In downtown NYC, the girls love nothing more than a bit of shopping. Especially shoe-shopping. And outfit-shopping. Oh, and handbag-shopping. Not to mention make-up and perfume shopping! It's a tough job but someone's got to do it. Will you find Kim amongst the luxury boutiques or spot Kylie in one of New York's many massive department stores?

Speaking of tough jobs, life in front of the cameras never stops and you need to look your best 24/7, whether it's in the photo studio or on the catwalk. Who will you find in the photo studio today? Khloe? Kendall?

When image is everything, the gym is a temple, so let's follow the family there. Even when they're sweating on the treadmill, never fear — they are still looking their blingtastic best.

Want to party like a Kardashian? Surely the Miami beaches are the best way to spot the family mixing with fellow megastars and dancing like no-one's watching. No-one except us, that is!

Bora Bora is a perfect getaway for this sun-loving family. It's beach or bust for Kourtney's tan. Smuggle yourself on board their private jet and check out their south-seas paradise hideaway, but make sure that Kim's earrings are firmly on!

Of course, there's no place like home. If you can get past security, then drop in on the Kardashian mansion for a big family party. With its sweeping staircase and grand hall, it's the perfect place for a family photo.

Now it's time for you to channel your inner paparazzi and check out all the hidden goings-on in these scenes. How many things can you spot from the Kardashian Kingdom?

Photo Studio

758936140

758936140

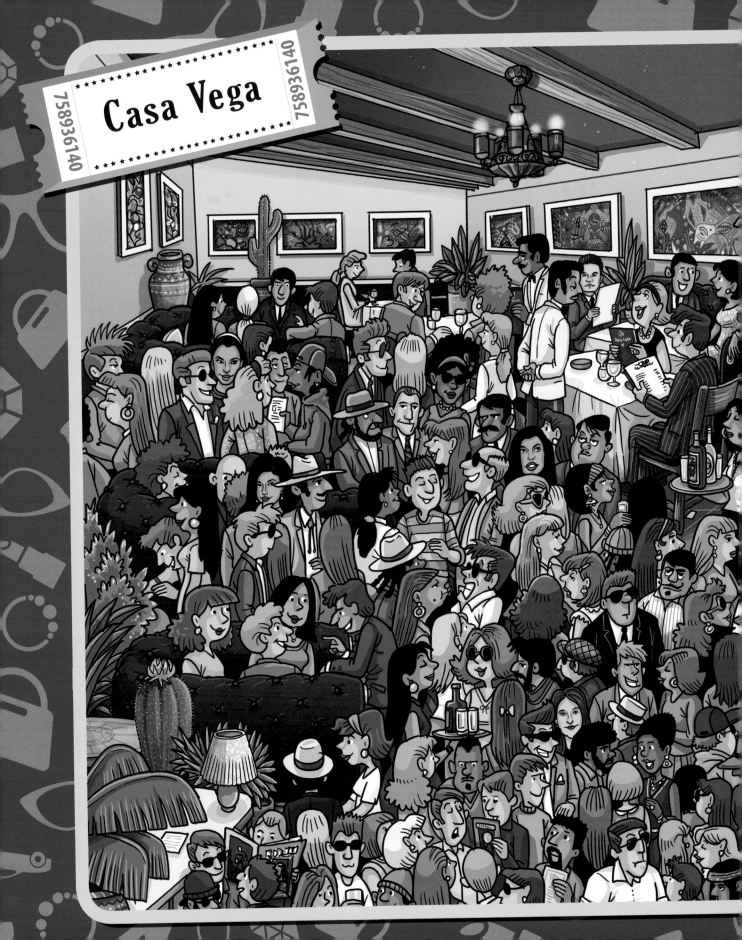

Casa Vega

758936140 758936140

At The Gym

758936140
758936140

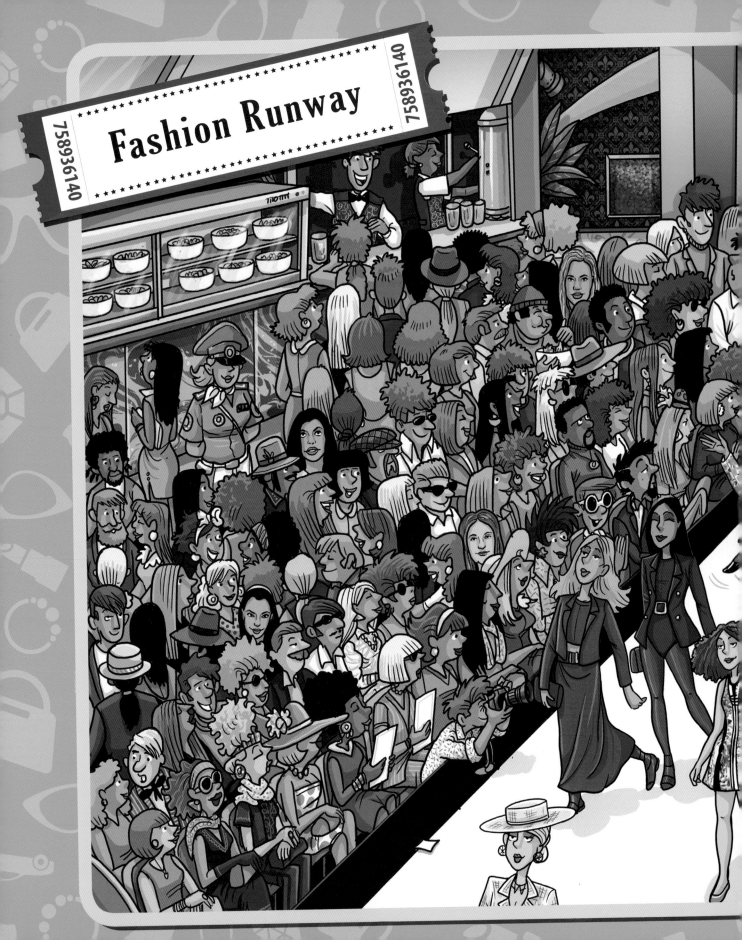

Palms Casino

758936140

758936140

Bora Bora

75893640

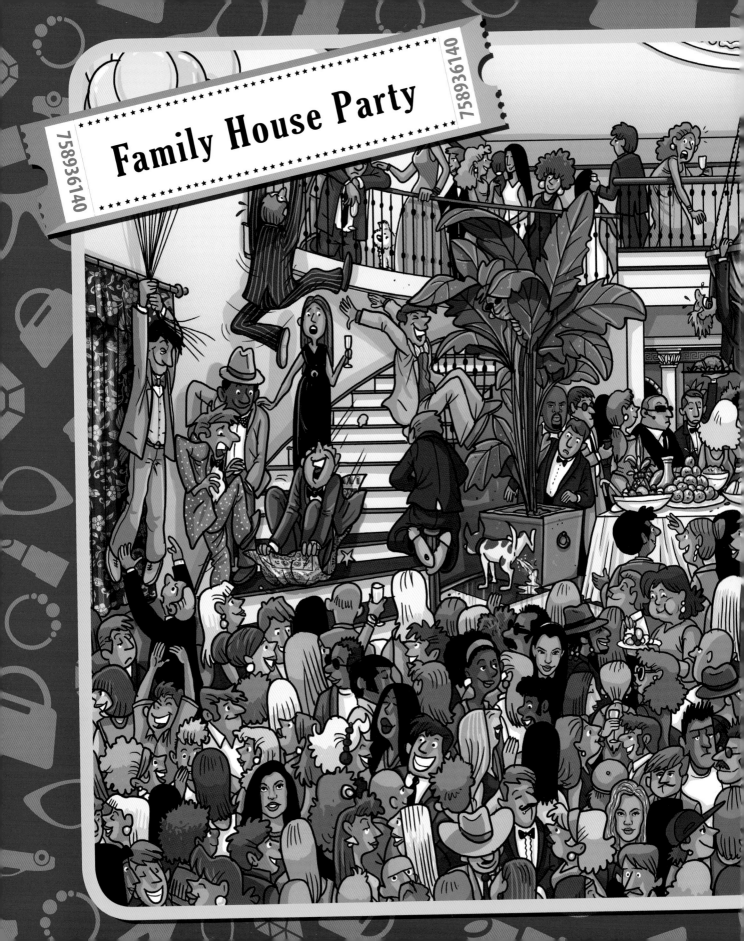

Family House Party

758936140

758936140

Kris Jenner —
The original 'Momager', Kris is the founder of the Kardashian brand. Mum to Kourtney, Kim, Khloe, and Rob Kardashian, Kylie and Kendall Jenner.

Caitlyn Jenner —
Before her 2015 gender transition, Caitlyn (born Bruce Jenner) was married to Kris for 14 years. A former Olympic Decathlon Champion, she is now a stylish TV celebrity.

Rob Kardashian —
Only son of Kris, Rob is best known for appearing with his family on KUWTK. His engagement to Blac Chyna had its own spin-off show.

Scott Disick —
Kourtney's on-off partner and father of her children, Scott is best known for some angry outbursts on KUWTK. The couple have now separated.

Kanye West —
Featured on KUWTK as Kim's husband, Kanye is an internationally renowned rapper known for some controversial and outspoken appearances in the media.

Ryan Seacrest —
Ryan got involved with the Kardashians when he struck a deal with Kris to film the family back in 2007. The rest, as they say, is history.

Corey Gamble —
Kris' boyfriend, the couple have had a few ups and downs since Corey's first appearances on KUWTK.